GOODGRAPHIA

blue

student manual

Writing & Spelling practice for letters, words and sentences

GOODGRAPHIA
blue
student manual

Writing & Spelling practice for letters, words and sentences

CICI COCO

www.thesentencelab.com

Author: Cici Coco
Designer/Illustrator: Molly Macfarlane

Copyright © 2021 Cici Coco
All rights reserved.
ISBN: 978-1-7369234-1-2

Contents

UNIT 1 3

UNIT 2 21

UNIT 3 39

UNIT 4 57

UNIT 5 75

UNIT 6 93

UNIT 7 111

UNIT 8 129

UNIT 9 147

UNIT 10 165

UNIT 11 183

UNIT 12 201

UNIT 13 219

UNIT 14 237

UNIT 15 255

UNIT 16 273

 **1** Copy

I sit in a pit.

Total Letters	Words / Min

2 Move

3 Write 63 Letters

1.

2.

3.

4.

5.

6.

7.

8.

9.

4 Spell by Sound

1.

2.

3.

4.

5.

6.

7.

8.

9.

5 Blocked or Open

1.

2.

3.

4.

5.

1 Move

2 Spell from Memory

1.

2.

3.

4.

5.

6.

3 Spell the Sound

1.   2.   3.   4.   5.   6.

7.   8.   9.   10.   11.   12.

4 Write 63 Letters

1.

2.

3.

4.

5.

6.

7.

8.

9.

6

5 Initial / Medial / Final

	initial	medial	final
1.			
2.			
3.			
4.			

6 Code

1.  I | sit .

2. Tip snips .

3. I spin .

4. Tip sits .

1 Move

2 Write 28 Letters

1.

2.

3.

4.

3 Build Derivatives

baseword	suffix	derivative
1.		
2.		
3.		
4.		

1. Tip

2. sits

4 Combine

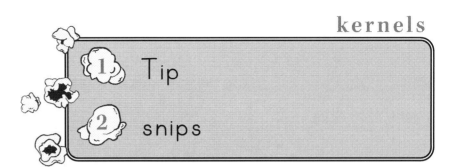

kernels

1 Tip

2 snips

5 Combine

1 Move

2 Spell by Sound

1. _____ _____ _____

2. _____ _____ _____

3. _____ _____ _____

4. _____ _____ _____

3 Spell by Memory

1. _____ _____ _____

2. _____ _____ _____

3. _____ _____ _____

4. _____ _____ _____

5. _____ _____ _____

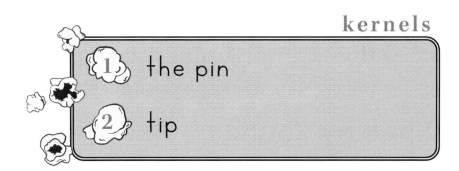

kernels

1 the pin

2 tip

4 Combine

1 I

2 see a pit

5 Combine

1 Move

 2 Unscramble

see a pin I

14

3 Expand

Word Min

Tip sits

My Words

UNIT 1

I sit and

My Words

1 Move

2 Write Your Own

pin	Word Min
tip	

My Words

3 Spell by Sound and Memory

1.

2.

3.

4.

5.

6.

7.

8.

9.

 **4** Copy

I sit in a pit.

Total Letters | Words / Min

1 Copy

A cat ran past.

Total Letters	Words / Min

2 Move

3 Write 63 Letters

1.

2.

3.

4.

5.

6.

7.

8.

9.

4 Spell by Sound

1.
2.
3.
4.
5.

 **5** Blocked or Open

1.
2.
3.
4.
5.

6.
7.
8.
9.

1 Move

2 Spell from Memory

1.

2.

3.

4.

5.

6.

3 Spell the Sound

1.   2.   3.   4.   5.   6.

7.   8.   9.   10.   11.   12.

4 Write 63 Letters

1.

2.

3.

4.

5.

6.

7.

8.

9.

5 Initial / Medial / Final

initial	medial	final
1.		
2.		
3.		
4.		

6 Code

1. [The cat | trips] .

2. A cat ran .

3. Pat plans .

4. The ants ran .

1 Move

2 Write 28 Letters

1.

2.

3.

4.

3 Build Derivatives

baseword	suffix	derivative
1.		
2.		
3.		
4.		

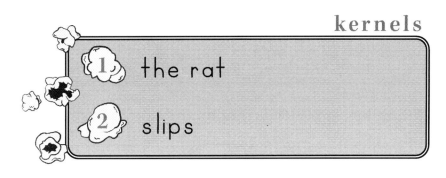

kernels

1 the rat

2 slips

4 Combine

1 the ant

2 trips

5 Combine

1 Move

2 Spell by Sound

1. _____ _____ _____

2. _____ _____ _____

3. _____ _____ _____

4. _____ _____ _____

3 Spell by Memory

1. _____ _____ _____

2. _____ _____ _____

3. _____ _____ _____

4. _____ _____ _____

5. _____ _____ _____

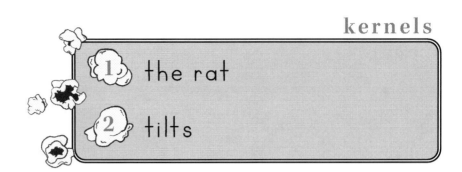

kernels

1 the rat

2 tilts

🍎 4 Combine

kernels

1 Cal

2 plants

5 Combine

kernels

1 Move

 2 Unscramble

spins cat the

3 Expand

Word Min

The cat sprints.

My Words

A cat ran and...

My Words

1 Move

2 Write Your Own

ants	Word Min
eye	

My Words

3 Spell by Sound and Memory

1.

2.

3.

4.

5.

6.

7.

8.

9.

4 Copy

A cat ran past.

Total Letters	Words / Min

1 Copy

A rat rips the pad.

Total Letters	Words / Min

2 Move

 3 Write 63 Letters

1.

2.

3.

4.

5.

6.

7.

8.

9.

4 Spell by Sound

1.
2.
3.
4.
5.
6.
7.
8.
9.

5 Blocked or Open

1.
2.
3.
4.
5.

1 Move

2 Spell from Memory

1.

2.

3.

4.

5.

6.

3 Spell the Sound

1. 2. 3. 4. 5. 6.

7. 8. 9. 10. 11. 12.

4 Write 63 Letters

1.

2.

3.

4.

5.

6.

7.

8.

9.

5 Initial / Medial / Final

initial	medial	final
1.		
2.		
3.		
4.		

6 Code

1. [The (tall) cat | limps].

2. A blue crab grabs .

3. A funny cat spins .

4. The tall man ran .

1 Move

2 Write 28 Letters

1.

2.

3.

4.

3 Build Derivatives

baseword   suffix   derivative

1.

2.

3.

4.

kernels

1. The clam sits.

2. The clam was blue.

4 Combine

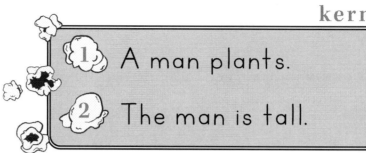

1 A man plants.

2 The man is tall.

5 Combine

1 Move

2 Spell by Sound

1. _____ _____ _____

2. _____ _____ _____

3. _____ _____ _____

4. _____ _____ _____

3 Spell by Memory

1. _____ _____ _____

2. _____ _____ _____

3. _____ _____ _____

4. _____ _____ _____

5. _____ _____ _____

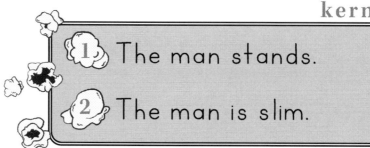

1. The man stands.

2. The man is slim.

4 Combine

1. A cat eats.

2. The cat is tan.

5 Combine

1 Move

 2 Unscramble

tan the drips rat

3 Expand

Word Min

Viv claps.

My Words

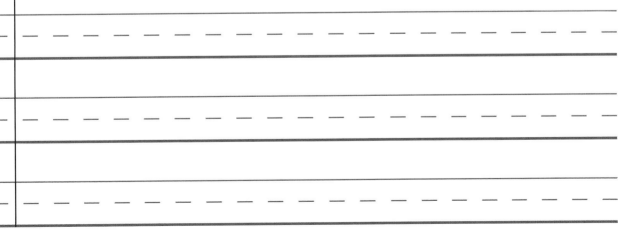

4 Expand

The tall man claps and...

1 Move

2 Write Your Own

camp	Word Min
rain	

My Words

3 Spell by Sound and Memory

1.

2.

3.

4.

5.

6.

7.

8.

9.

 **4 Copy**

A rat rips the pad.

Total Letters	Words / Min

 **Copy**

The wind can bring mist.

Total Letters	Words / Min

2 Move

3 Write 63 Letters

1.

2.

3.

4.

5.

6.

7.

8.

9.

4 Spell by Sound

1.

2.

3.

4.

5.

6.

7.

8.

9.

5 Blocked or Open

1.

2.

3.

4.

5.

1 Move

2 Spell from Memory

1.

2.

3.

4.

5.

6.

3 Spell the Sound

1.　　2.　　3.　　4.　　5.　　6.

7.　　8.　　9.　　10.　　11.　　12.

4 Write 63 Letters

1.

2.

3.

4.

5.

6.

7.

8.

9.

5 Initial / Medial / Final

initial	medial	final
1.		
2.		
3.		
4.		

6 Code

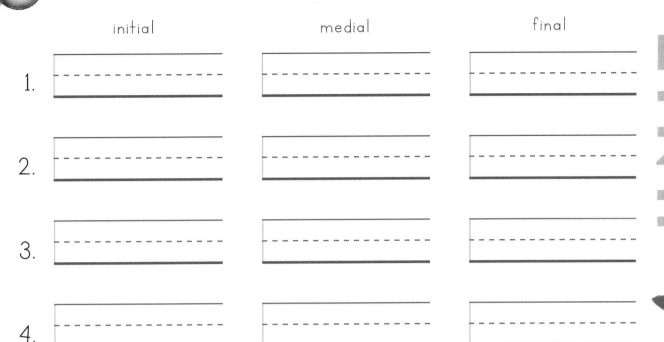

1. [The (old) cat | napped (on the mat) .]

2. The tan cat naps on the pants.

3. A tall man sat on the mat.

4. The big girl stamped on the map.

1 Move

2 Write 28 Letters

1.

2.

3.

4.

3 Build Derivatives

baseword	suffix	derivative
1.		
2.		
3.		
4.		

62

kernels

1. The girl landed.

2. The girl was funny.

3. She landed in the sand.

4) Combine

kernels

1. The crab ran.

2. The crab was blue.

3. It ran in the sand.

5 Combine

64

1 Move

2 Spell by Sound

1. _____ _____ _____

2. _____ _____ _____

3. _____ _____ _____

4. _____ _____ _____

3 Spell by Memory

1. _____ _____ _____

2. _____ _____ _____

3. _____ _____ _____

4. _____ _____ _____

5. _____ _____ _____

kernels

1. The twins swam.

2. The twins were tall.

3. They swam to Dad.

4 Combine

kernels

1. The rams ran.

2. There are two rams.

3. They ran to dry land.

5 Combine

1 Move

 2 Unscramble

rips damp the map The

twig

3 Expand

Word Min

I slept in a camp.

My Words

4 Expand

The old ram sprinted and...

1 Move

2 Write Your Own

swing | Word Min
puppy |

My Words

3 Spell by Sound and Memory

1.

2.

3.

4.

5.

6.

7.

8.

9.

4 Copy

The wind can bring mist.

Total Letters	Words / Min

1 Copy

The bag sat in the big

van.

Total Letters	Words / Min

2 Move

 3 Write 63 Letters

1.

2.

3.

4.

5.

6.

7.

8.

9.

4 Spell by Sound

1. _____

2. _____

3. _____

4. _____

5. _____

6. _____

7. _____

8. _____

9. _____

5 Blocked or Open

1. _____

2. _____

3. _____

4. _____

5. _____

1 Move

2 Spell from Memory

1.

2.

3.

4.

5.

6.

3 Spell the Sound

1. 2. 3. 4. 5. 6.

7. 8. 9. 10. 11. 12.

4 Write 63 Letters

1.

2.

3.

4.

5.

6.

7.

8.

9.

78

5 Initial / Medial / Final

 initial   medial   final

1.

2.

3.

4.

6 Code

1. [The girl | spins [on the (pink) mat]].

2. The cat pulled on the old string.

3. The crab dripped on the tan sand.

4. The rat ran to the green bush.

1 Move

2 Write 28 Letters

1.

2.

3.

4.

3 Build Derivatives

baseword	suffix	derivative
1.		
2.		
3.		
4.		

kernels

 The cat sat at the bank.

 The bank was damp.

4 Combine

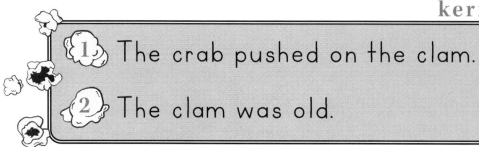

1. The crab pushed on the clam.

2. The clam was old.

5 Combine

1 Move

2 Spell by Sound

1. _____ _____ _____

2. _____ _____ _____

3. _____ _____ _____

4. _____ _____ _____

3 Spell by Memory

1. _____ _____ _____

2. _____ _____ _____

3. _____ _____ _____

4. _____ _____ _____

5. _____ _____ _____

UNIT 5

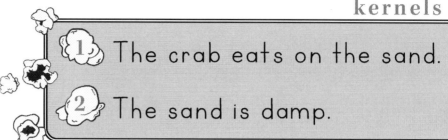

kernels

1. The crab eats on the sand.

2. The sand is damp.

4 Combine

kernels

1. Her pants ripped on a twig.

2. The twig was green.

5 Combine

1 Move

 2 Unscramble

at sprinted the The ram

old bull

3 Expand

Brin drank at the sink.

My Words

4 Expand

The mink limped to the bush and...

Move

 Write Your Own

| mix | Word Min |
| kid | |

My Words

3 Spell by Sound and Memory

1. _____ _____ _____

2. _____ _____ _____

3. _____ _____ _____

4. _____ _____ _____

5. _____ _____ _____

6. _____ _____ _____

7. _____ _____ _____

8. _____ _____ _____

9. _____ _____ _____

 **4** Copy

The bag sat in the big

van.

Total Letters	Words / Min

 **1** Copy

The crab is in his sink.

Total Letters	Words / Min

2 Move

3 Write 63 Letters

1.

2.

3.

4.

5.

6.

7.

8.

9.

4 Spell by Sound

1.

2.

3.

4.

5.

6.

7.

8.

9.

5 Blocked or Open

1.

2.

3.

4.

5.

1 Move

2 Spell from Memory

1. _____   _____   _____

2. _____   _____   _____

3. _____   _____   _____

4. _____   _____   _____

5. _____   _____   _____

6. _____   _____   _____

3 Spell the Sound

1. ____ 2. ____ 3. ____ 4. ____ 5. ____ 6. ____

7. ____ 8. ____ 9. ____ 10. ____ 11. ____ 12. ____

UNIT 6

4 Write 63 Letters

1.

2.

3.

4.

5.

6.

7.

8.

9.

5 Initial / Medial / Final

<table>
<thead>
<tr><th>initial</th><th>medial</th><th>final</th></tr>
</thead>
<tbody>
<tr><td>1.</td><td></td><td></td></tr>
<tr><td>2.</td><td></td><td></td></tr>
<tr><td>3.</td><td></td><td></td></tr>
<tr><td>4.</td><td></td><td></td></tr>
</tbody>
</table>

6 Code

1. [The bird | flapped its wings].

2. The girl lifted the hat.

3. The bats flapped their wings.

4. Dad missed the pass.

1 Move

2 Write 28 Letters

1.

2.

3.

4.

3 Build Derivatives

baseword	suffix	derivative
1.		
2.		
3.		
4.		

1 The bird flaps.

2 The bird is blue.

3 It flaps its wings.

4 Combine

kernels

1. The girl spills.

2. The girl is sad.

3. She spills her milk.

5 Combine

1 Move

2 Spell by Sound

1.

2.

3.

4.

3 Spell by Memory

1.

2.

3.

4.

5.

1. The girl fixes the ham.

2. The girl was tall.

3. The ham was good.

 4 Combine

kernels

1. The man lifted.

2. The man was tall.

3. He lifted the fan.

5 Combine

1 Move

 2 Unscramble

a clasped The clam

crab

Word Min

Finn spilled the milk.

My Words

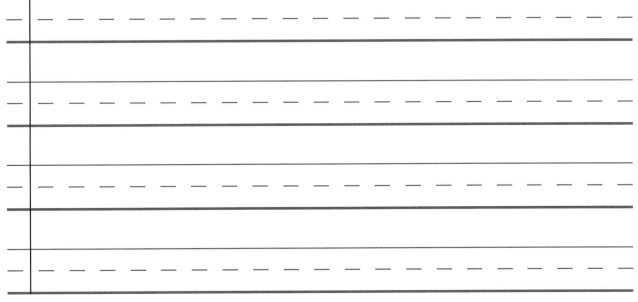

Word Min

The blue bird tapped
the twig and...

My Words

1 Move

2 Write Your Own

hill | Word Min
happy |

My Words

3 Spell by Sound and Memory

1.

2.

3.

4.

5.

6.

7.

8.

9.

4 Copy

The crab is in his sink.

 **1** Copy

I got a grip on the

sharp gem.

Total Letters	Words / Min

2 Move

3 Write 63 Letters

1.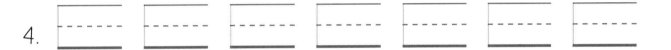

2.

3.

4.

5.

6.

7.

8.

9.

4 Spell by Sound

1.

2.

3.

4.

5.

6.

7.

8.

9.

5 Blocked or Open

1.

2.

3.

4.

5.

1 Move

2 Spell from Memory

1. _____ _____ _____

2. _____ _____ _____

3. _____ _____ _____

4. _____ _____ _____

5. _____ _____ _____

6. _____ _____ _____

3 Spell the Sound

1. _____ 2. _____ 3. _____ 4. _____ 5. _____ 6. _____

7. _____ 8. _____ 9. _____ 10. _____ 11. _____ 12. _____

4 Write 63 Letters

1.

2.

3.

4.

5.

6.

7.

8.

9.

5 Initial / Medial / Final

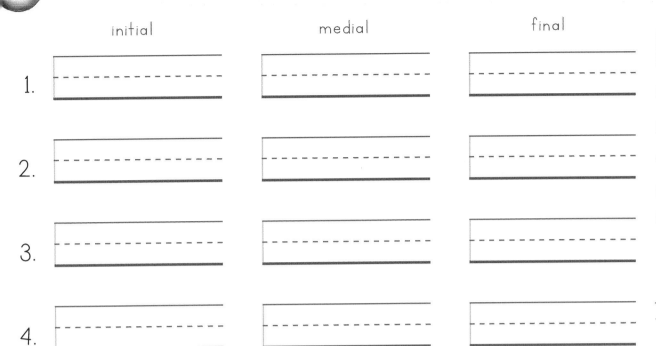

	initial	medial	final
1.			
2.			
3.			
4.			

6 Code

1. [On the (front) sink , Jax | fixed the (warm) shrimp .]

2. On the big ship, Cash dragged the cold crab.

3. At swim camp, her son swam two laps.

4. On the red map, Viv put a yellow pin.

1 Move

2 Write 28 Letters

1.

2.

3.

4.

3 Build Derivatives

baseword	suffix	derivative
1.		
2.		
3.		
4.		

kernels

1. Tim stomps the grass.

2. He is at the marsh.

3. The grass is green.

4 Combine

1. Jin drank the milk.

2. She drank at the sink.

3. The milk was cold.

5 Combine

1 Move

2 Spell by Sound

1.

2.

3.

4.

3 Spell by Memory

1.

2.

3.

4.

5.

kernels

1. Jax filled the jar.

2. Jax was in the car.

3. The jar was tall.

4 Combine

kernels

 1 Ash dragged the lamp.

2 He dragged it from the car.

3 The lamp was big.

 5 Combine

1 Move

 2 Unscramble

yellow van Jill grabbed
the the card In

3 Expand

Mark wishes for a ball.

My Words

 **Expand**

In class Bill sang a sad

song and...

124

Move

Write Your Own

| sharp | Word Min |
| some | |

My Words

3 Spell by Sound and Memory

1.

2.

3.

4.

5.

6.

7.

8.

9.

 **4** Copy

I got a grip on the

sharp gem.

Total Letters | Words / Min

1 Copy

His son had to come in from the wind.

2 Move

 3 Write 63 Letters

1.

2.

3.

4.

5.

6.

7.

8.

9.

4 Spell by Sound

1. _____

2. _____

3. _____

4. _____

5. _____

6. _____

7. _____

8. _____

9. _____

5 Blocked or Open

1. _____

2. _____

3. _____

4. _____

5. _____

1 Move

2 Spell from Memory

1. _____ _____ _____

2. _____ _____ _____

3. _____ _____ _____

4. _____ _____ _____

5. _____ _____ _____

6. _____ _____ _____

3 Spell the Sound

1. _____ 2. _____ 3. _____ 4. _____ 5. _____ 6. _____

7. _____ 8. _____ 9. _____ 10. _____ 11. _____ 12. _____

4 Write 63 Letters

1.

2.

3.

4.

5.

6.

7.

8.

9.

5 Initial / Medial / Final

initial	medial	final
1.		
2.		
3.		
4.		

6 Code

1. [We | parked the car and the van].

2. He lifted the cards and the prints.

3. The ram stamped the grass and the bush.

4. Dad filled the jar and the dish.

1 Move

2 Write 28 Letters

1.

2.

3.

4.

3 Build Derivatives

baseword	suffix	derivative
1.		
2.		
3.		
4.		

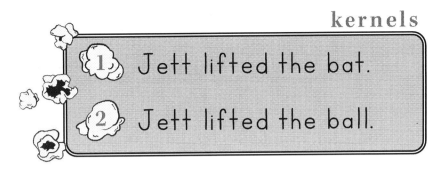

kernels

1. Jett lifted the bat.

2. Jett lifted the ball.

4 Combine

UNIT 8

1. Pat asked Mark.

2. Pat asked Max.

5 Combine

1 Move

2 Spell by Sound

1. _____ _____ _____

2. _____ _____ _____

3. _____ _____ _____

4. _____ _____ _____

3 Spell by Memory

1. _____ _____ _____

2. _____ _____ _____

3. _____ _____ _____

4. _____ _____ _____

5. _____ _____ _____

kernels

1 Cal snapped the twig.

2 Cal snapped the plant.

4 Combine

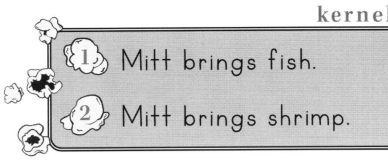

kernels

1. Mitt brings fish.

2. Mitt brings shrimp.

5. Combine

1 Move

 2 Unscramble

yams mint and Mitt

sees the the

3 Expand

Brin fixed a dish and a drink.

Expand

The bird flapped her
wings in the wind and...

My Words

1 Move

2 Write Your Own

| yard | Word Min |
| honked | |

My Words

3 Spell by Sound and Memory

1.

2.

3.

4.

5.

6.

7.

8.

9.

4 Copy

His son had to come in
from the wind.

Total Letters	Words / Min

 **Copy**

Mom will shop with this cart.

Total Letters	Words / Min

2 Move

3 Write 63 Letters

1.

2.

3.

4.

5.

6.

7.

8.

9.

4 Spell by Sound

1. _____

2. _____

3. _____

4. _____

5. _____

6. _____

7. _____

8. _____

9. _____

5 Blocked or Open

1. _____

2. _____

3. _____

4. _____

5. _____

1 Move

2 Spell from Memory

1.

2.

3.

4.

5.

6.

3 Spell the Sound

1.   2.   3.   4.   5.   6.

7.   8.   9.   10.   11.   12.

4 Write 63 Letters

1.

2.

3.

4.

5.

6.

7.

8.

9.

5 Initial / Medial / Final

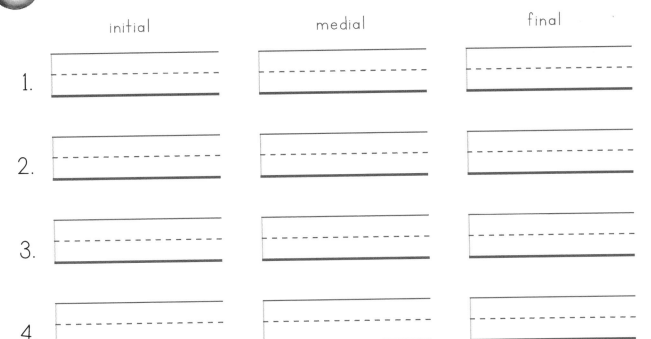

	initial	medial	final
1.			
2.			
3.			
4.			

6 Code

1. The girl and her dad sang a new song.

2. The ram and the ox had a long drink.

3. The crab and the shrimp swam two laps.

4. The dad and his son mopped the old ship.

1 Move

2 Write 28 Letters

1.

2.

3.

4.

3 Build Derivatives

baseword	suffix	derivative
1.		
2.		
3.		
4.		

kernels

1. Brad planned the trip.

2. Tim planned the trip.

3. The trip was long.

4 Combine

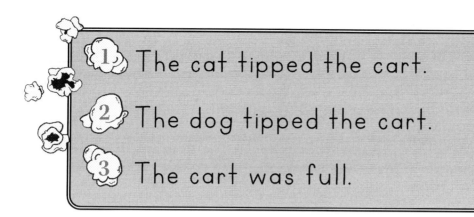

kernels

1. The cat tipped the cart.

2. The dog tipped the cart.

3. The cart was full.

5 Combine

1 Move

2 Spell by Sound

1.

2.

3.

4.

3 Spell by Memory

1.

2.

3.

4.

5.

kernels

1. Viv drank milk.

2. The milk was warm.

3. Star drank milk.

4 Combine

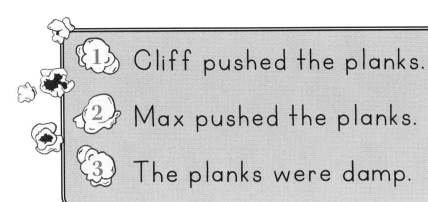

1. Cliff pushed the planks.

2. Max pushed the planks.

3. The planks were damp.

5 Combine

1 Move

 2 Unscramble

fish Sol got a Thad big

and

3 Expand

Word Min

Mom and Dad spotted

a...

My Words

4 Expand

Tom and Bill spotted a green frog and...

My Words

160

1 Move

2 Write Your Own

moth	Word Min
shop	

My Words

3 Spell by Sound and Memory

1.

2.

3.

4.

5.

6.

7.

8.

9.

 **4 Copy**

Mom will shop with this

cart.

Total Letters	Words / Min

1 Copy

I kept a cart in the shed.

Total Letters	Words / Min

2 Move

3 Write 63 Letters

1.

2.

3.

4.

5.

6.

7.

8.

9.

4 Spell by Sound

1. _____

2. _____

3. _____

4. _____

5. _____

6. _____

7. _____

8. _____

9. _____

5 Blocked or Open

1. _____

2. _____

3. _____

4. _____

5. _____

1 Move

2 Spell from Memory

1.

2.

3.

4.

5.

6.

3 Spell the Sound

1.   2.   3.   4.   5.   6.

7.   8.   9.   10.   11.   12.

4 Write 63 Letters

1.

2.

3.

4.

5.

6.

7.

8.

9.

168

5 Initial / Medial / Final

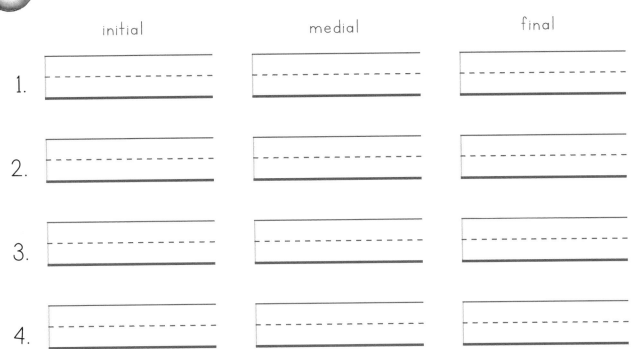

initial	medial	final
1.		
2.		
3.		
4.		

6 Code

1. [Brit and Keb | fixed the fish in the sink] .

2. Cash and Bret pulled the fish

   into the ship .

3. Her son and his pal put the jar

   on the cart .

4. Viv and Nell put the string in the van .

1 Move

2 Write 28 Letters

1.

2.

3.

4.

3 Build Derivatives

baseword	suffix	derivative
1.		
2.		
3.		
4.		

1. Mim pets the cat.

2. Peg pets the cat.

3. Mim and Peg were at camp.

4. Combine

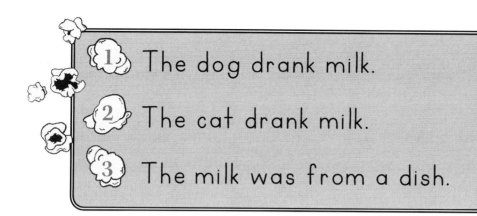

1. The dog drank milk.

2. The cat drank milk.

3. The milk was from a dish.

5 Combine

 Move

2 Spell by Sound

1.

2.

3.

4.

3 Spell by Memory

1.

2.

3.

4.

5.

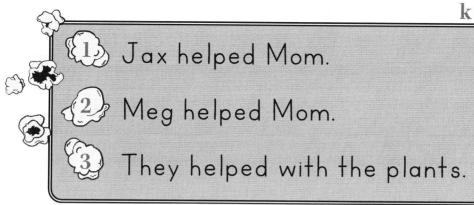

1. Jax helped Mom.

2. Meg helped Mom.

3. They helped with the plants.

4 Combine

kernels

1. Ash dragged the plants.

2. Sol dragged plants.

3. They dragged them to the yard.

5 Combine

1 Move

2 Unscramble

on and shelf Thad the

Jim string the put

(3) Expand

Mark and Jan ask for...

My Words

4 Expand

Bill and Tom sang a

song...

1 Move

2 Write Your Own

yell shed	Word Min

My Words

3 Spell by Sound and Memory

1.

2.

3.

4.

5.

6.

7.

8.

9.

4 Copy

I kept a cart in the shed.

Total Letters	Words / Min

1 Copy

The ball was an inch on top of my head.

Total Letters	Words / Min

2 Move

 3 Write 63 Letters

1.

2.

3.

4.

5.

6.

7.

8.

9.

4 Spell by Sound

1.
2.
3.
4.
5.
6.
7.
8.
9.

5 Blocked or Open

1.
2.
3.
4.
5.

1 Move

2 Spell from Memory

1. _____ _____ _____

2. _____ _____ _____

3. _____ _____ _____

4. _____ _____ _____

5. _____ _____ _____

6. _____ _____ _____

3 Spell the Sound

1. _____ 2. _____ 3. _____ 4. _____ 5. _____ 6. _____

7. _____ 8. _____ 9. _____ 10. _____ 11. _____ 12. _____

4 Write 63 Letters

1.

2.

3.

4.

5.

6.

7.

8.

9.

5 Initial / Medial / Final

initial	medial	final
1.		
2.		
3.		
4.		

6 Code

1. The chimp and the cub | ran and tugged
   on the grass.

2. A crab and a clam swam and swam in the pond.

3. A shrimp and a crab grabbed a clam in the pond.

4. A fox and an ox ran in the barn.

UNIT 11

1 Move

2 Write 28 Letters

1.

2.

3.

4.

3 Build Derivatives

baseword	suffix	derivative
1.		
2.		
3.		
4.		

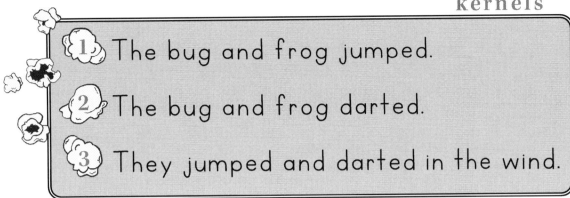

1. The bug and frog jumped.

2. The bug and frog darted.

3. They jumped and darted in the wind.

4. Combine

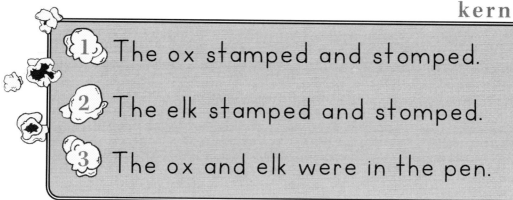

kernels

1. The ox stamped and stomped.

2. The elk stamped and stomped.

3. The ox and elk were in the pen.

5 Combine

1 Move

2 Spell by Sound

1.

2.

3.

4.

3 Spell by Memory

1.

2.

3.

4.

5.

UNIT 11

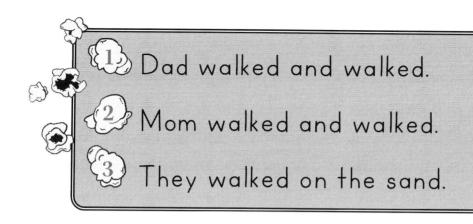

kernels

1. Dad walked and walked.

2. Mom walked and walked.

3. They walked on the sand.

4 Combine

kernels

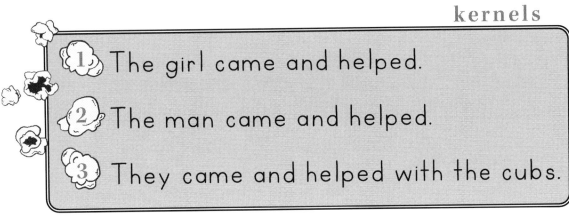

1. The girl came and helped.

2. The man came and helped.

3. They came and helped with the cubs.

5 Combine

1 Move

 2 Unscramble

frog The red and the
and frog jumped in
green spring hopped

3 Expand

Word Min

The small bat and the big bat flapped.

My Words

4 Expand

The cub and the frog...

1 Move

2 Write Your Own

squid	Word Min
eight	

My Words

3 Spell by Sound and Memory

1.

2.

3.

4.

5.

6.

7.

8.

9.

4 Copy

The ball was an inch on top of my head.

Total Letters	Words / Min

1 Copy

He will shout if he can get in to the shed.

Total Letters	Words / Min

2 Move

3 Write 63 Letters

1.

2.

3.

4.

5.

6.

7.

8.

9.

4 Spell by Sound

1. _____

2. _____

3. _____

4. _____

5. _____

6. _____

7. _____

8. _____

9. _____

5 Blocked or Open

1. _____

2. _____

3. _____

4. _____

5. _____

1 Move

2 Spell from Memory

1.

2.

3.

4.

5.

6.

3 Spell the Sound

1. 2. 3. 4. 5. 6.

7. 8. 9. 10. 11. 12.

4 Write 63 Letters

1.

2.

3.

4.

5.

6.

7.

8.

9.

204

5 Initial / Medial / Final

initial   medial   final

1.

2.

3.

4.

6 Code

1. [The cow| found grass and ate it] .

2. The kid found a pal and played tag .

3. The man caught a trout and ate it .

4. Gus thanked his mom and hugged his dad .

1 Move

2 Write 28 Letters

1.

2.

3.

4.

3 Build Derivatives

baseword	suffix	derivative
1.		
2.		
3.		
4.		

1 Mom got cash.

2 Mom put it in her bag.

4 Combine

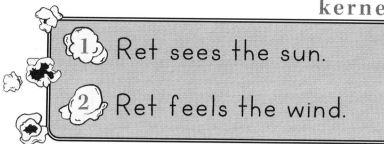

kernels

1 Ret sees the sun.

2 Ret feels the wind.

5 Combine

1 Move

2 Spell by Sound

1.

2.

3.

4.

3 Spell by Memory

1.

2.

3.

4.

5.

UNIT 12

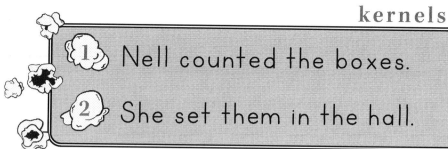

kernels

1. Nell counted the boxes.

2. She set them in the hall.

4 Combine

kernels

1. Max caught two trout.

2. Max netted eight crabs.

5 Combine

Move

 Unscramble

played Ash caught got

tag and

3 Expand

Word Min

Chip and Sol gulped.

My Words

4 Expand

Em hummed a song and...

1 Move

2 Write Your Own

cloud gulp	Word Min

My Words

3 Spell by Sound and Memory

1.

2.

3.

4.

5.

6.

7.

8.

9.

4 Copy

He will shout if he can
get in to the shed.

Total Letters	Words / Min

1 Copy

My cart is now full,
and I can not push it.

Total Letters	Words / Min

2 Move

3 Write 63 Letters

1.

2.

3.

4.

5.

6.

7.

8.

9.

4 Spell by Sound

1.
2.
3.
4.
5.
6.
7.
8.
9.

5 Blocked or Open

1.
2.
3.
4.
5.

1 Move

2 Spell from Memory

1.

2.

3.

4.

5.

6.

3 Spell the Sound

1.   2.   3.   4.   5.   6.

7.   8.   9.   10.   11.   12.

4 Write 63 Letters

1.

2.

3.

4.

5.

6.

7.

8.

9.

5 Initial / Medial / Final

initial	medial	final

1.

2.

3.

4.

6 Code

1. The proud kid sang and chanted in the play.

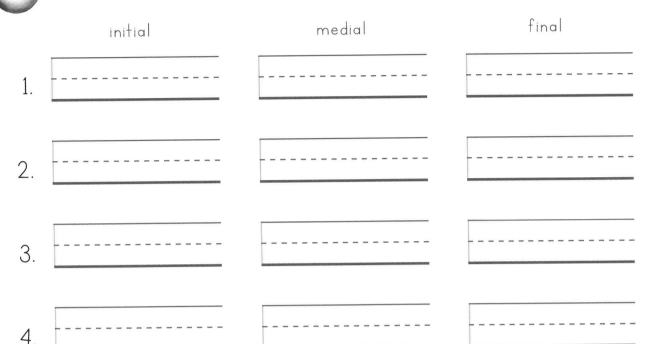

2. The old wood split and warped in the damp .

3. The brown pup crept and looked

   at the crowd .

4. My left foot slipped and knocked

   on the wood .

1 Move

2 Write 28 Letters

1.

2.

3.

4.

3 Build Derivatives

baseword	suffix	derivative
1.		
2.		
3.		
4.		

kernels

1. The elk stood.

2. The elk looked.

3. It was at the brook.

4. The elk was brown.

4 Combine

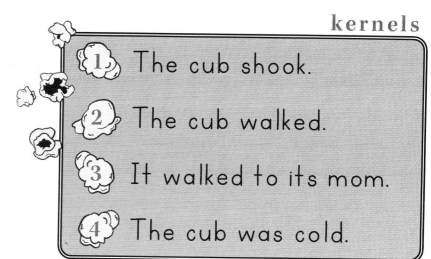

1. The cub shook.

2. The cub walked.

3. It walked to its mom.

4. The cub was cold.

5. Combine

1 Move

2 Spell by Sound

1. _____ _____ _____

2. _____ _____ _____

3. _____ _____ _____

4. _____ _____ _____

3 Spell by Memory

1. _____ _____ _____

2. _____ _____ _____

3. _____ _____ _____

4. _____ _____ _____

5. _____ _____ _____

Chip planned.

Chip mapped.

He planned and mapped the path.

The path was to the town.

 4 Combine

kernels

The girl fell.

The girl knocked her knee.

She knocked it on the wood.

She was next.

5 Combine

1 Move

 2 Unscramble

big at dog a found cat

and The it howled

3 Expand

Word Min

The small sloth hung
and slept on the branch.

My Words

4 Expand

The small sloth ate...

1 Move

2 Write Your Own

took shout	Word Min

My Words

3 Spell by Sound and Memory

1.

2.

3.

4.

5.

6.

7.

8.

9.

4 Copy

My cart is now full,

and I can not push it.

Total Letters	Words / Min

Her dear mom pushed the cart near that spot in the yard.

Total Letters	Words / Min

 **2** Move

 **3** Write 63 Letters

1.

2.

3.

4.

5.

6.

7.

8.

9.

4 Spell by Sound

1. _____

2. _____

3. _____

4. _____

5. _____

6. _____

7. _____

8. _____

9. _____

5 Blocked or Open

1. _____

2. _____

3. _____

4. _____

5. _____

1 Move

2 Spell from Memory

1. _____

2. _____

3. _____

4. _____

5. _____

6. _____

3 Spell the Sound

1. _____ 2. _____ 3. _____ 4. _____ 5. _____ 6. _____

7. _____ 8. _____ 9. _____ 10. _____ 11. _____ 12. _____

4 Write 63 Letters

1.

2.

3.

4.

5.

6.

7.

8.

9.

240

5 Initial / Medial / Final

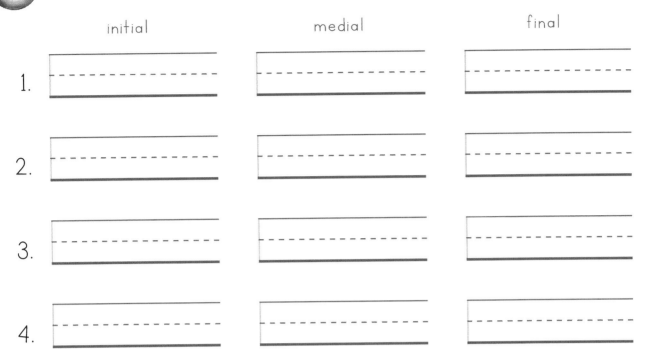

	initial	medial	final
1.			
2.			
3.			
4.			

6 Code

1. [The (brown) fly | landed], and [the

   (yellow) bug | hopped].

2. The work gear fell , and the old spear split .

3. A small bug tugs , and a red ant pushes .

4. The small pug walked , and the big hound ran .

1 Move

2 Write 28 Letters

1.

2.

3.

4.

3 Build Derivatives

baseword	suffix	derivative
1.		
2.		
3.		
4.		

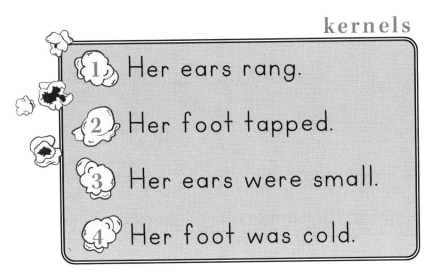

1. Her ears rang.

2. Her foot tapped.

3. Her ears were small.

4. Her foot was cold.

4 Combine

1. The dog howled.

2. The pup yipped.

3. The dog was strong.

4. The pup was happy.

5. Combine

1 Move

2 Spell by Sound

1.

2.

3.

4.

3 Spell by Memory

1.

2.

3.

4.

5.

1. The mug shook.

2. The cup slid.

3. The mug was red.

4. The cup was yellow.

 4 Combine

kernels

1. The girl knocked.

2. Her mom rang the bell.

3. The girl was happy.

4. Her mom was kind.

5 Combine

1 Move

 2 Unscramble

strong stood and the

the small bent elm ash

248

3 Expand

The hook bent.

My Words

4 Expand

Her strong clamp held the wood and...

1 Move

2 Write Your Own

her knee	Word Min

My Words

3 Spell by Sound and Memory

1.

2.

3.

4.

5.

6.

7.

8.

9.

4 Copy

Her dear mom pushed
the cart near that spot
on the lawn.

Total Letters	Words / Min

 **1** Copy

I can fix the tool box
on the bench.

Total Letters	Words / Min

2 Move

3 Write 63 Letters

1.

2.

3.

4.

5.

6.

7.

8.

9.

255

4 Spell by Sound

1. _____

2. _____

3. _____

4. _____

5. _____

6. _____

7. _____

8. _____

9. _____

5 Blocked or Open

1. _____

2. _____

3. _____

4. _____

5. _____

 Move

2 Spell from Memory

1.

2.

3.

4.

5.

6.

3 Spell the Sound

1.   2.   3.   4.   5.   6.

7.   8.   9.   10.   11.   12.

4 Write 63 Letters

1.

2.

3.

4.

5.

6.

7.

8.

9.

258

5 Initial / Medial / Final

	initial	medial	final
1.			
2.			
3.			
4.			

6 Code

1. [Ash | fixed the box], and [Fern | put it

   [on the shelf]].

2. Jon shook the shoe , and the dog grabbed it .

3. Grant likes books , and Tess likes kites .

4. Kent rides a bike , and Chad rides a trike .

1 Move

2 Write 28 Letters

1.
2.
3.
4.

3 Build Derivatives

baseword	suffix	derivative
1.		
2.		
3.		
4.		

kernels

1. Liv will buy chives.

2. Brad will buy ripe plums.

4 Combine

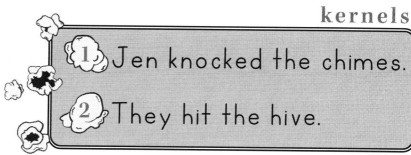

1. Jen knocked the chimes.

2. They hit the hive.

5 Combine

1 Move

2 Spell by Sound

1.

2.

3.

4.

3 Spell by Memory

1.

2.

3.

4.

5.

kernels

1. Nell ran a mile.

2. Mim ran two laps.

🍎 4 Combine

264

kernels

1. Dev cooked the fish on the grill.

2. Tess put lime on the fish.

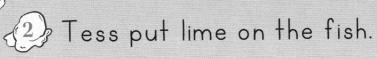

5 Combine

1 Move

 2 Unscramble

his cleaned dirt in eye

got and Mom Keb it out

3 Expand

Word Min

Jax started a fire in the pit.

My Words

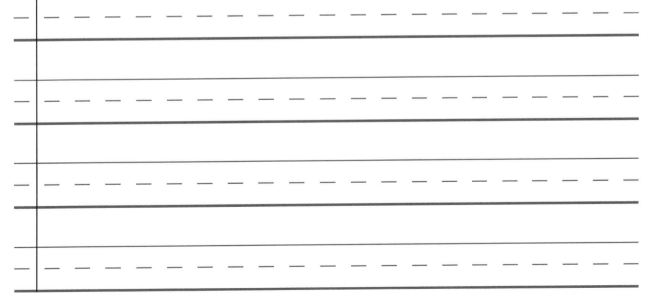

4 Expand

Word Min

I will read eight books and...

My Words

Move

 Write Your Own

| laugh | Word Min |
| shoe | |

My Words

3 Spell by Sound and Memory

1.

2.

3.

4.

5.

6.

7.

8.

9.

 Copy

I can fix the tool box
on the bench.

Total Letters	Words / Min

The short book was

quite good.

Total Letters	Words / Min

 2 Move

 3 Write 63 Letters

1.

2.

3.

4.

5.

6.

7.

8.

9.

4 Spell by Sound

1.

2.

3.

4.

5.

6.

7.

8.

9.

5 Blocked or Open

1.

2.

3.

4.

5.

1 Move

2 Spell from Memory

1.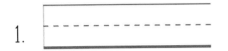

2.

3.

4.

5.

6.

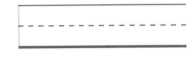

3 Spell the Sound

1. _____ 2. _____ 3. _____ 4. _____ 5. _____ 6. _____

7. _____ 8. _____ 9. _____ 10. _____ 11. _____ 12. _____

4 Write 63 Letters

1.

2.

3.

4.

5.

6.

7.

8.

9.

5 Initial / Medial / Final

initial	medial	final

1.

2.

3.

4.

6 Code

1. [At night], Mom | reads books], and [Bess
   joins her].

2. In the storm , Bev knitted a scarf , and Sam
   cooked lunch .

3. At night , Art eats dinner , and Ash cleans
   the dishes .

4. In the nest , a bird cleans its beak , and
   an owl cleans her wing .

1 Move

2 Write 28 Letters

1.

2.

3.

4.

3 Build Derivatives

baseword	suffix	derivative
1.		
2.		
3.		
4.		

kernels

 1. Roy ate corn.

 2. Peg drank tea.

 3. They ate and drank at the feast.

4. Combine

UNIT 16

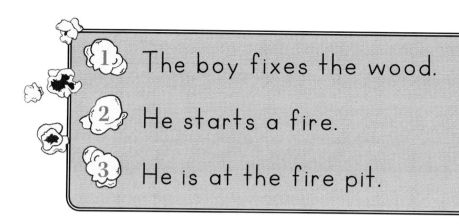

1. The boy fixes the wood.

2. He starts a fire.

3. He is at the fire pit.

5 Combine

1 Move

2 Spell by Sound

1.
2.
3.
4.

3 Spell by Memory

1.
2.
3.
4.
5.

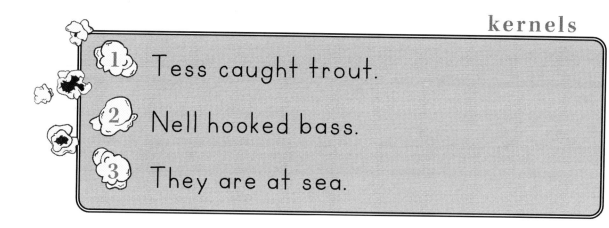

1. Tess caught trout.

2. Nell hooked bass.

3. They are at sea.

4. Combine

282

kernels

1. Mom buys the toys.

2. Dad hides the toys.

3. They are at the shop.

5 Combine

Move

 Unscramble

the cows farm and
Beth the On pigs spots
hears the Lin

3 Expand

The milk spilled.

My Words

4 Expand

She caught a fish and...

1 Move

2 Write Your Own

| toy
short | Word Min |

My Words

3 Spell by Sound and Memory

1. _____ _____ _____

2. _____ _____ _____

3. _____ _____ _____

4. _____ _____ _____

5. _____ _____ _____

6. _____ _____ _____

7. _____ _____ _____

8. _____ _____ _____

9. _____ _____ _____

 **4** Copy

The short book was

quite good.

Total Letters	Words / Min

Made in the USA
Columbia, SC
06 April 2025

56237475R00161